FIVE DELICIOUS 5 MUFFINS

Written by Cheryl Blinston

Illustrated by Larry Moore

5 steaming muffins. The baker ate 1.

4 hot muffins.

Paul ate 1.

3 warm muffins.

Vicki ate 1.

$$3 - 1 = 2$$

2 cool muffins.

Fifi ate 1.

$$2-1=1$$

1 cold muffin.

The baker ate 1 more.

$$1 - 1 = 0$$

0 muffins.

"Ding!" went the timer. 5 more hot muffins.